GRIT & GOLD

CELEBRATING

NATIONAL LIBRARY
OF AUSTRALIA
PUBLISHING

50 YEARS

FOREWORD

The National Library of Australia is a place of great vitality. The building hums with activity as we add new material to our collections, as we run the digital services that connect Australians everywhere with our collections, and as visitors come to our reading rooms and galleries to discover stories of Australia's history, culture and identity.

Our collections cover the full range of human endeavour in the fields of visual art, literature, politics, economics, law, science and innovation, from across an increasingly diverse Australia. Perhaps less well known, but no less vital, is our collection of sporting imagery and memorabilia.

The National Library's exhibition *Grit and Gold: Tales from a Sporting Nation* contains images and objects that tell Australian stories through an athletic lens, and captures an essential part of the Australian spirit. Here are moments of triumph, passion, heartbreak, endeavour and endurance played out on a national or international stage. And the quiet (and not so quiet!) moments of courage, camaraderie and community that happen at local fields, pools and courts around the country every week. So many of us—even those not naturally athletically blessed—have grown up on sporting fields, cheered our children on from the sidelines or enjoyed that fabulous feeling of being part of a huge crowd at the MCG or a Sydney Test. I have incredibly clear memories of going to the 1975 Australia–West Indies Test in Perth, in the days of the Chappells, Lillee, Thompson and Marsh, of Richards, Lloyd and Holding. We got horribly sunburned in Perth's December sun—and it was worth it!

This exhibition companion contains a curated selection of *Grit and Gold* items, from a photograph of the New South Wales Koori Knockout to the first Melbourne Cup trophy, a poster of Hubert Opperman and his Malvern Star, a fan-shaped lithograph of an early Australian Rules Football game and a joyful image of the Matildas' Sam Kerr performing her trademark goal celebration.

A favourite piece for me is a photograph of a women's cricket team from Tilba Tilba in New South Wales, taken around 1905 by amateur documentary photographer William Henry Corkhill. As incongruous as those ankle-length white dresses look in the middle of a paddock, these women were enjoying a physical pastime that had been practised by women in Australia since at least 1874, when the first match was held in Bendigo. At the time the photograph was taken, the Victorian Women's Cricket Association was running a competition with 21 teams. There are plenty of other surprises in *Grit and Gold*.

The interdisciplinary collections in the National Library contain stories for everyone. I invite you to explore Australia's sporting heritage through *Grit and Gold*.

Dr Marie-Louise Ayres FAHA
Director-General
National Library of Australia

TALES FROM A SPORTING NATION

Sport is a storytelling machine. And for Australians that machine is prolific. The Australian popular imagination is crowded with stories drawn from sporting contests. Whether it is Ash Barty winning the Australian Open in 2022 or the 'Bodyline series' of 1932–1933, there are almost too many to tell. These stories, and many more, are explored in the National Library of Australia's exhibition *Grit and Gold: Tales of a Sporting Nation.*

Some sporting moments go beyond providing a memorable anecdote; they change the way the nation sees itself. Cathy Freeman's victory in the 400-metre race at the Sydney Olympics is one such moment. Freeman was already famous for having carried both the Aboriginal and Australian flags after her victory in the 200-metre final at the 1994 Commonwealth Games. Carrying both flags reflected her pride in being Indigenous and in being Australian. For many Australians, this celebration of her victory symbolised the possibility of reconciliation between First Australians and European Australians. At the 2000 Olympics, Freeman was selected to light the Olympic Cauldron at the beginning of the Games. The image of her standing with an Olympic torch surrounded by fire became a symbol of a new Australian identity that recognised the centrality of Indigenous people to the Australian story. All that remained for this moment to become part of the national imagination was for her to run a winning race. Commentator Bruce McAvaney exalted in Freeman's convincing victory: 'What a legend ... what a champion!' Co-commentator and Australian sprint legend Raelene Boyle expressed what many Australians felt: 'What a relief!'

What is it about sport that makes it so good at generating stories? Sporting contests provide a space for compelling narratives to be created. The constraints and rules of each contest, and the passion of the participants, allow the audience to identify with the athlete and care about the outcome. The possibility of victory or defeat means that there is something at stake in each contest. And the physical danger inherent in many sports amplifies this sense of jeopardy. The emotions and pain expressed on players' faces provides a very raw and powerful experience for fans. As each sporting contest unfolds, there is the possibility for heroes to appear, to overcome obstacles and to return home victorious. Similarly, villains on the opposing side can thwart the hopes of a team and its fans. Following the contest is an immersive experience in which the rest of the world disappears. There is suspense and surprise, there is exaltation and despair. You are taken on a journey that has a definite end, even though you might not always like the result.

The narrative power of sport is recognised in the glut of sporting documentaries that fill our streaming services. Whether it is ESPN's *30 for 30* series of classic sporting moments, Amazon's *The Test* about the redemption of the Australian Test cricket team after the infamous sandpaper incident or Netflix's *Last Dance* about basketballer Michael Jordan and the Chicago Bulls' NBA '3-peat'—and the ABC's *Australian Story* about why Australian star Luc Longley was left out of the documentary—there is clearly a strong demand for sporting stories.

The recent popularity of these documentaries is a reminder of the way sporting stories are told and retold, endlessly circulating among fans. Some of these escape their code of origin and come to symbolise much more than a fleeting moment on a sportsground. These stories can be inscribed with a broader meaning for the individual, neighbourhood or nation. They can come to be part of a shared set of experiences that bind a community together.

This use of sport to help build a sense of community has been a potent force in Australia. In a nation created not as an expression of a political ideal, but rather as a compromise to facilitate trade, defence and migration, sport has always served to define Australian identity. Stories of sporting achievement helped establish the worth of Australia, both for its sports-crazed citizens and for the wider world. Aussies love to boast that they 'punch above their weight' in international sporting competitions. Whether it is dominating in cricket (sometimes), winning gold at the Olympics (most of the time) or exceeding expectations at the Football World Cup (passionately hoped for), the triumph of Australian athletes is seen as proof positive of Australia's success as a nation.

Australia's interest in sporting achievement began to manifest soon after the arrival of the First Fleet in 1788. The convicts, soldiers and settlers who came to Australia to set up an outpost for the British Empire brought with them the sporting culture of eighteenth-century

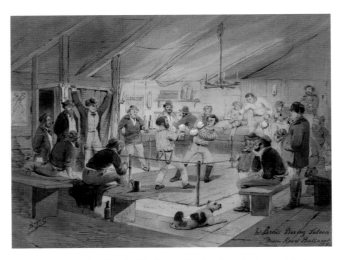

S.T. GILL (1818–1880), *McLaren's Boxing Saloon, Main Road, Ballarat*, 1854

Britain. As the precarious colonial settlements grew into prosperous communities, opportunities for leisure and sport increased. Hunting, horseracing, cricket, pedestrianism, rowing and boxing were just some of the British sports that found a new home in Australia. These pastimes became a focus of colonial life, and the athletes who excelled at them quickly became some of the most celebrated personalities in colonial society.

These new arrivals in Australia knew they were moving to a land that was already occupied. They had little or no knowledge of the types of sport played by its First Nations people. John Heaviside Clark published a short book in 1813 entitled *Field Sports, Etc., Etc., of the Native Inhabitants of New South Wales*. Clark's introductory essay provides some superficial observations on what he describes as the 'field sports' of the Indigenous people of New South Wales. The essay reflects the racist attitudes of the settlers of the period, but it also makes clear that the 'inhabitants' saw the land as theirs. He quotes a 'chief' from Parramatta who, when arguing with a settler about his use of fire near a cornfield, declared: 'You know we must have our fire, the country is *ours*, you must take care of your corn'. Clark provides illustrations of First

Nations people hunting and fishing, and praises their skill. He describes the lethal design of their spears, and the prowess the hunters displayed in their use: 'Their expertise is truly surprising; they rarely fail to hit the mark at fifty or sixty yards'. While Clark was impressed by the athletic accomplishment of the spear-throwing, he did not engage with how hunting was not a sport, but rather a key way that First Nations people gathered food.

Reading Clark's account leaves us with more questions than answers about the nature and extent of sport in Australia prior to 1788. Other than his brief observations, made from a European perspective, we have no direct evidence concerning what sport may have meant for First Australians. Clark's focus on hunting and fishing, both pastimes which the settlers also enjoyed, shows how he was drawn to the most relatable aspects of First Nations culture. While claiming to provide a guide to the original inhabitants of New South Wales, Clark's book reveals how little the colonisers truly understood the First Nations peoples.

While we know little about Indigenous sport in the early days of colonisation, First Australians had a major impact on the subsequent development of Australian sport. Australian Rules football (AFL), for example, drew inspiration from Indigenous games. There were stories of a game played in western Victoria called *marn grook*, in which Indigenous people kicked a skin football. This predated the codification of AFL. First Australians also faced significant barriers to participation in British sport. The lack of resources, prohibitions on competing and racist attitudes made it difficult for them to play sport. Despite these obstacles, First Nations people would prove to be very adept at mastering the games of the colonisers. Many of today's sporting champions, such as Cathy Freeman, Ash Barty and footballers Adam Goodes and Latrell Mitchell, proudly celebrate their Indigenous heritage.

As the Australian colonies matured, sporting contests with England took on an outsized significance in settler colonial society. While it is something of a cliché to say that the English dismissed the Australian colonies as a dumping ground for convicts and younger sons, there is a definite sense that colonial Australians felt they had a lot to prove. Victory over England on the sporting field was the ideal way to prove self-worth. This desire to best the mother country at its own games is reflected in the story of the Ashes. This small urn, allegedly holding the ashes of some burned cricket bails, has come to represent one of the most famous cricketing rivalries in the world. After an Australian side defeated England, on English soil, an obituary notice was placed in *The Sporting Times*: 'In Affectionate Remembrance of English Cricket, which died at The Oval on 29th August, 1882 ... N.B.—*The body will be cremated and the ashes taken to Australia*'. The English captain, Ivo Bligh, vowed to regain the 'Ashes' and, on a tour the following summer, England defeated Australia two Tests to one. Bligh was presented with a small urn—most likely, an emptied perfume bottle—inscribed 'The Ashes', marking the resumption of England's cricketing supremacy. With each new Ashes series, the English–Australian rivalry has been layered with cricketing anecdotes, making it one of the most storied sports trophies in the world.

With Federation in 1901, Australia formally became a nation. Many Australians, however, still identified strongly with Britain and with their home states. Sporting champions would help erode this parochialism and forge a stronger sense of national identity. Two athletes from the early twentieth century, boxer Les Darcy and cricketer Victor Trumper, stand out as trailblazing national heroes. For both, the key to their impact on the national imagination lay in their premature deaths.

Darcy was a boxer from Maitland, New South Wales. Born in 1895 into a working-class Irish Catholic family, and apprenticed as a blacksmith, he would become a hero for Irish Australians. His rapid rise through the Australian boxing ranks led to interest from promoters in the United States. He left Australia in 1916, on the eve of the first

I.F. WEEDON (1864–1924), *English and Australian Cricketers: Great Match, England vs Australia, Played at Lord's Cricket Ground, London, 19–21 July 1886*, 1887

conscription referendum, prompting some newspapers to accuse him of 'shirking'. Unable to secure championship fights owing to the controversy surrounding his departure from Australia, Darcy fell ill in Memphis, Tennessee, after a botched dental procedure. He died of septicaemia on 24 May 1917. He was just 21 years of age. His embalmed body was returned to Australia, and his funeral saw thousands of boxing fans pay their respects. Darcy instantly became the personification of what could have been. In a trope that would often be repeated in Australian sporting culture, he was lauded as a champion who had been cruelly robbed of the chance to prove his greatness.

Like Darcy, Victor Trumper also died at an early age. Trumper first came to prominence in the 1890s when he represented New South Wales and eventually emerged as a champion batter for Australia. After he scored 11 centuries in the 1902 Australian tour of England, the cricketing bible *Wisden* declared Trumper the 'best batsman in the world'. He finished his first-class career in 1914, having accumulated 16,939 runs in 255 matches, with his highest score being 300 not out. In an age when wickets were not covered during rain, creating almost impossible batting conditions at times, Trumper achieved a remarkable average of 44.58.

A key element of Trumper's popularity with the Australian sporting public stemmed from his status in England. His performance in Anglo-Australian Tests proved that he was as good, if not better, than the cricketers of the mother country. His teammate Clem Hill observed that Trumper 'has done as much for Australia as anyone, and in England he is the one Australian batsman they long to watch'.

If the first 50 years of Australian and English cricket rivalry reflect the desire of a young nation for recognition from the mother country, the 'Bodyline series' of 1932–1933 can be seen as akin to the moment when a teenager rejects the actions of a cruel parent. 'Bodyline' was the term used to describe the tactics employed by the English team to subdue Australia's batting line-up, and in particular its all-time batting hero, Don Bradman. It involved targeting the leg stump with intimidating fast-rising deliveries. The batter had to quickly choose whether to duck, allow the ball to hit their body or strike it with their bat. Additional fielders were placed on the leg side to catch the ball should the hapless batter try to play a shot. While the strategy did restrict the flow of runs, it was condemned as unsporting by many players, journalists and fans. During the third Test at the Adelaide Oval, English fast bowler Harold Larwood hit Australian captain Bill Woodfull on the chest with a rising delivery. The game was stopped while Woodfull recovered. The English captain, Douglas Jardine, was overheard as he loudly congratulated Larwood's delivery. Spectators grew increasingly restless as the English persisted with their leg attack. Woodfull bravely continued his innings, but was hit again on the body, and eventually succumbed for just 22 runs. The next day, newspapers across Australia quoted Woodfull as saying, 'There are two teams out there. One is trying to play cricket and the other is not'.

The bitter controversy that surrounded the 'Bodyline series' is the perfect example of how sporting moments can be absorbed into Australia's national mythology. In this story, Bradman and Woodfull are local heroes, standing bravely against an English bully. Jardine can be seen as an aloof Englishman—a caricature of an Oxbridge gentleman looking down on Australia. This combined with the fact that the series was unfolding at the height of the Great Depression meant that it could become a proxy for Australian–British relations. The Bank of England had called on Australian state and federal governments to cut public expenditure to pay back English loans. And New South Wales Premier Jack Lang had campaigned for the suspension of interest payments on loans, eventually leading to his dismissal. In this context of economic distress and political crisis, Jardine's ruthless tactics could be seen as emblematic of an arrogant and disdainful British attitude towards Australia.

In postwar Australia, the 1956 Olympics are remembered as a moment of national pride in sporting achievement. It was the first time the Olympics had been staged in the Southern Hemisphere. Australian athletes did extremely well, winning a total of 35 medals, including 13 gold. Star performers included Betty Cuthbert (gold medals in the 100-metre and 200-metre sprints, as well as in the 4 x 100-metre relay) and Shirley Strickland (gold in the 80-metre hurdles and the 4 x 100-metre relay). Australia also dominated the swimming, winning all the men's and women's freestyle events, including Dawn Fraser's first gold medal in the 100-metre freestyle and Murray Rose's three gold medals in the 400-metre and 1,500-metre freestyle and in the 4 x 200-metre freestyle relay.

The Games were held at a time of heightened international tensions. In the weeks prior to the opening ceremony Israel, France and Britain invaded Egypt following the Egyptian government's decision to nationalise the Suez Canal. The Soviet Union had

DAVID MOORE (1927–2003), *Portrait of Dawn Fraser, Melbourne,* 1963

also recently ruthlessly crushed the pro-democracy uprising in Hungary. It was in this context that 17-year-old Chinese-Australian John Ian Wing wrote to the organising committee of the Games in Melbourne suggesting that all athletes should march together as part of the closing ceremony: 'During the march there will be only one nation. War, politics and nationality will be all forgotten, what more could anybody want, if the whole world could be made as one nation?' The letter struck a chord with the organisers, and plans were quickly put in place for athletes to enter the Melbourne Cricket Ground from the eastern end of the stadium, not in their national teams, but as a single group. Australian stars Strickland, Cuthbert and Fraser proudly led the march. And so, at the end of what came to be known as the 'Friendly Games', national allegiances were put aside in an expression of solidarity among athletes.

The idealism of the march of athletes would soon be tempered by the capacity of sport to generate money. Cricket was the arena in which these commercial imperatives first began to play out. When the Australian Cricket Board rejected an offer from media proprietor Kerry Packer for the broadcast rights for Test cricket, it unwittingly triggered a major shift in Australian sport. Packer responded by establishing the World Series Cricket competition in 1977. After two seasons of parallel international competitions a compromise was negotiated—and Packer achieved his goal of obtaining the cricket broadcast rights.

The World Series Cricket model which Packer developed provided a template that could be applied to other sports. The two most obvious candidates were the major winter football competitions in Australia: the Victorian Football League (VFL) and the New South Wales Rugby League (NSWRL). While these competitions were based in Melbourne and Sydney respectively, they both had significant national followings. Partially forewarned by the establishment of World Series Cricket, the administrators of both competitions began a process of expansion and professionalisation in the early 1980s. Competitions that had been parochial and suburban for decades were about to be transformed into major national sports businesses.

The brave new world of professional sport would not always prove a happy one, however. The grand narrative of Australia as a 'tough but fair' sporting nation was challenged in Cape Town, South Africa, in 2018, when television cameras captured Australian opener Cameron Bancroft surreptitiously using sandpaper to tamper with a cricket ball. This action shocked a nation used to hearing stories of Australia's noble sporting achievements. The ensuing controversy consumed Australian cricket, resulting in the suspension of Australian captain Steve Smith and vice-captain David Warner for 12 months. Bancroft was suspended for nine months. Even in this moment of infamy, however, the 'sandpaper incident' quickly became a cautionary tale of great players being led astray. This 'tragedy' was felt beyond the world of cricket with then Australian Prime Minister Malcolm Turnbull describing it as beyond belief that the Australian cricket team could be involved in cheating. Sport once again demonstrated its capacity to generate stories that would quickly become part of Australia's shared historical memory.

As we enter the third decade of the twenty-first century, sport continues to generate new stories that bring Australians together. One of the most striking recent examples has been the professionalisation of women's elite sport. Professional women's national leagues have been established in soccer (2008) cricket (2015), netball (2016), Australian Rules football (2017) and rugby league (2018). These sports have also negotiated broadcast and sponsorship agreements that brought much needed cash into their codes. While the pay gap has not fully closed, elite women's sport has been transformed.

When looking at changes in sport over the last 200 years, you can see that it provides a window into Australian history. Whether it concerns the emergence of a distinct Australian national identity in the nineteenth century, the growth of professional sport in the twentieth century or the rise of elite women's competitions more recently, sport gives us an invaluable insight into major changes in our society and culture. The National Library of Australia is a place where these sporting stories can be found and retold for future generations. The printed material, artworks, ephemera, personal papers and oral histories held by the Library provide a storehouse of memories for all Australians to cherish.

Dr Guy Hansen
Director, Exhibitions, National Library of Australia

THE GAME BEGINS

The convicts, soldiers and settlers who came to Australia to set up an outpost of the British Empire brought with them the sporting culture of eighteenth-century Britain. As the colonial settlements grew, opportunities for leisure and sport increased. British sports, including hunting, horseracing, cricket, pedestrianism, rowing and boxing, found a new home in Australia. These pastimes became a focus of colonial life, and the athletes who excelled at them quickly became some of the most celebrated personalities in colonial society.

EDWARD ROPER (1832–1909), *A Kangaroo Hunt under Mount Zero, the Grampians, Victoria, Australia*, 1880

KANGAROO HUNTING

European interest in shooting kangaroos can be traced as far back as Cook's *Endeavour* voyage in 1770. Hunting clubs appeared from the 1830s and provided opportunities for wealthy settlers to shoot kangaroos, drawing on the British tradition of hunting. In places such as Victoria, hunts were carried out on horseback with rifles, and with the assistance of hounds. A popular theme in colonial art, pictures of kangaroo hunts evolved in the nineteenth century, from idealised images that often featured settlers and First Nations people to depictions of settlers shown dominating both kangaroos and the land.

WALTER G. MASON (1820–1866) *The Flying Pieman, a Celebrated Sydney Pedestrian*, 1807

'THE FLYING PIEMAN'

William Francis King emigrated to New South Wales from London in 1829. In 1834, he went into business as an itinerant pieman around Hyde Park and Circular Quay. At Circular Quay, he offered his pies for sale to passengers boarding the Parramatta ferry, then ran with the remaining unsold pies to Parramatta, where he offered them for sale to the same passengers as they disembarked.

Between 1842 and 1851, King accomplished a range of athletic feats, such as walking 2,630 kilometres in 39 days, racing the Windsor-to-Sydney mail coach on foot (and twice beating it), and covering 402 kilometres in 10 days in Maitland.

THE FLYING PIEMAN, A CELEBRATED SYDNEY PEDESTRIAN.

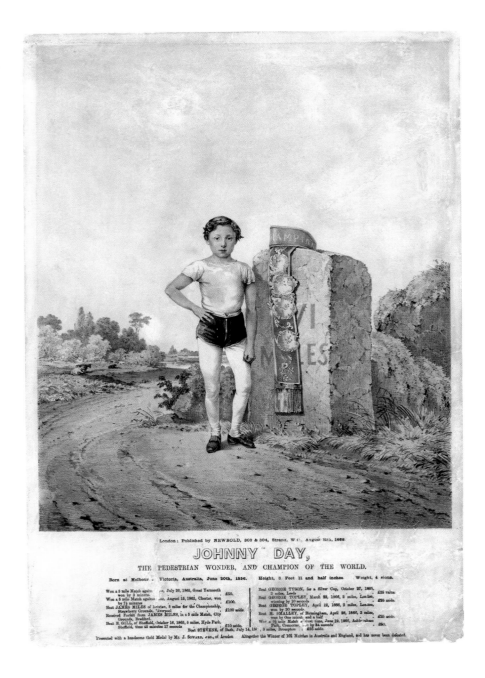

London: Published by NEWBOLD, 303 & 304, Strand, W.C., August 11th, 1866.

JOHNNY DAY,

THE PEDESTRIAN WONDER, AND CHAMPION OF THE WORLD.

Born at Melbourne, Victoria, Australia, June 20th, 1856.   Height, 3 Feet 11 and half inches   Weight, 4 stone.

Won a 5 mile Match against ..., July 26, 1865, Great Yarmouth
  won by 3 minutes
Won a 5 mile Match against ..., August 15, 1865, Chester, won   £50.
  by 7½ minutes
Beat JAMES MILES of ..., 5 miles for the Championship,   £100.
  Strawberry Grounds, Liverpool
Received Forfeit from JAMES MILES, in a 5 mile Match, City   £100 aside.
  Grounds, Bradford
Beat E. GILL, of Sheffield, October 16, 1865, 5 miles, Hyde Park,   £10 aside.
  Sheffield, time 45 minutes 17 seconds
Beat STEVENS, of Bath, July 14, 18...

Beat GEORGE TYSON, for a Silver Cup, October 27, 1865,   £25 value.
  2 miles, Leeds
Beat GEORGE TOPLEY, March 22, 1866, 3 miles, London,   £25 aside.
  winning by 10 seconds
Beat GEORGE TOPLEY, April 12, 1866, 2 miles, London,   £25 aside.
  won by 20 seconds
Beat H. SMALLEY, of Birmingham, April 28, 1866, 2 miles,   £25 aside.
  won by One minute and a half
Won a 3 mile Match against Best time, June 19, 1866, Ashbyculham   £50.
  Park, Crosscourse ... by 34 seconds   £50.
  3 miles, Brompton   £25 aside.

Presented with a handsome Gold Medal by Mr. J. Soward, jun., of London   Altogether the Winner of 101 Matches in Australia and England, and has never been defeated.

ARTIST UNKNOWN,
The Pedestrian Wonder and Champion of the World, 1866

'THE AUSTRALIAN WONDER'

Johnny Day was a world-champion juvenile walker who competed in Australia and London, winning 101 walking matches by age 10. Competitive walking, or 'pedestrianism' as it was known, became a popular working-class British, American and Australian pastime in the nineteenth century. Walkers would race each other over a set distance, or individually against the clock. Spectators paid a fee to watch and often wagered on the outcome. By the late 1860s, Day was working as a jockey. In 1870, aged just 14, he won the Melbourne Cup on Nimblefoot.

ADAM LINDSAY GORDON (1833–1870), *Mount Gambier Grand National,* c.1861

HORSEMAN AND POET

Adam Lindsay Gordon emigrated from England to Adelaide in 1853. He joined the mounted police before becoming a horse-breaker and steeplechase rider. Gordon wrote 'bush ballads' informed by white settler bush culture, including horses. These interests are also seen in his informal sketches, such as this image of a steeplechase event at Mount Gambier, where he competed and lived, on and off. Today he is better remembered for his influence on Australian poetry (as the only Australian represented in Poet's Corner, Westminster Abbey, London) than for his mixed success as a horseman.

J. RYAN, *Flemington Racecourse from the Footscray Side of Salt Water River, Victoria,* c.1845

A DAY AT THE RACES

The spectacle of horseracing often draws leisure seekers as much as it does race enthusiasts. Since ancient times, crowds have gathered to watch horseraces. In Australia, Flemington Racecourse in Victoria has a rich history as the heart of the racing industry, notably as host of the Melbourne Cup and associated fashion competitions and carnivals. Horseraces have taken place in the area since the 1840s, some two decades before the Melbourne Cup was first held. Races, as shown in this painting, provided an opportunity for community gatherings.

BATCHELDER & CO., *The First Melbourne Cup Trophy*, 1865

THE RACE THAT STOPS THE NATION

Traditionally, at 3pm on the first Tuesday of November, Australians pause for the running of the Melbourne Cup. Held at the Flemington Racecourse in Victoria, it is considered the world's richest two-mile race for thoroughbreds, with a purse of $8,000,000 in 2022. First run in 1861, the race was originally two miles (3,219 metres), but this was rounded down to 3,200 metres in 1972 after the introduction of the metric system.

The first trophy was introduced in 1865. The ornate nature of the silver trophy, which was manufactured in England, reflects the prestige of winning this race. Today many Australians still follow the Melbourne Cup. However, changing attitudes to horseracing have contributed to waning interest in the event.

CHARLES KERRY (1857–1928), *Miss Yan Ski Jumping, Snowy Mountains, New South Wales*, c.1900

FROM MINERS TO SKIERS

In the 1880s, Margaret Yan and her siblings entered—and often won—races at the annual Snow Shoe Carnival in Kiandra, in the Snowy Mountains. In 1894, Margaret won both ladies' races, while her brothers George and Frank were winners and placegetters in other events.

She won the ladies' race again in 1895 and was described in the *Cooma Express* as 'a perfect artist on shoes'. Snowshoeing and skiing were popular sports for goldminers and their families when they were unable to work due to the frozen ground in the Australian Alps during the late 1800s and early 1900s. Initially segregated from European skiers, the Chinese were skilled competitors.

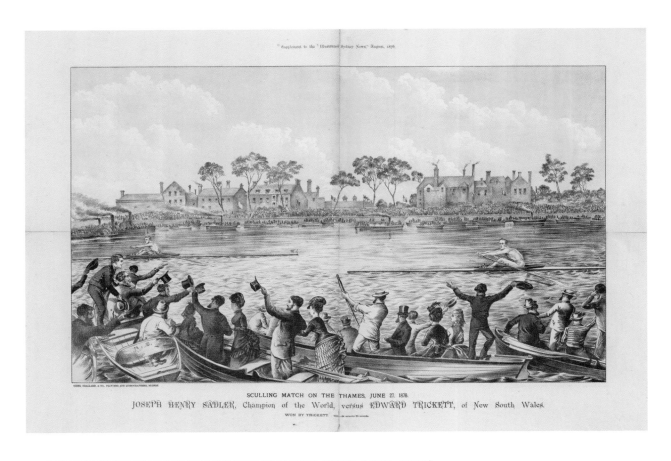

GIBBS, SHALLARD, & CO., PRINTERS AND LITHOGRAPHERS, SYDNEY.

SCULLING MATCH ON THE THAMES, JUNE 27, 1876.
JOSEPH HENRY SADLER, Champion of the World, versus EDWARD TRICKETT, of New South Wales.
WON BY TRICKETT

EUGENE MONTAGU 'MONTY' SCOTT (ILLUSTRATOR, 1835–1909); GIBBS, SHALLARD & CO. (PRINTERS AND LITHOGRAPHERS), *Sculling Match on the Thames, June 27 1876, Joseph Henry Sadler, Champion of the World, vs Edward Trickett, of New South Wales,* 1876

OUR FIRST WORLD CHAMPION

In 1876, Edward 'Ned' Trickett made history when he won the World Sculling Championships. Representing the colony of New South Wales, he became the first world sporting champion from Australia. Trickett defeated Joseph Sadler on the Thames course (Putney to Mortlake) in England. He won the next two world championships, in 1877 and 1879, both of which were held at Parramatta, but was defeated on the Thames in 1880. Racing from age 10, Trickett contributed to the popularity and success of Australian rowing in the late colonial period.

ARTIST UNKNOWN, *Sculling Race on River, Dent Royal Hotel*, c.1870

SPORT ON THE RIVER

Rowing was a popular sport in colonial Australia. While we don't know who painted this scene, or whether it depicts a real race, the work does capture the community atmosphere of rowing events at the time. The location might be Smythesdale (near Ballarat, Victoria), which had a Royal Hotel in the 1860s–1870s (it burnt down in 1877). A New Year's fete held in 1870 included a sculling (rowing) race. The fete included other recreation activities, providing an opportunity for people to gather and celebrate the new year.

S.T. GILL (1818–1880), *McLaren's Boxing Saloon, Main Road, Ballarat*, 1854

BRITISH BOXING

Britain had a long tradition of prize-fighting in the eighteenth and nineteenth centuries. Bare-knuckle fights that lasted for many rounds were not uncommon. Champions of the sport were held up as the personification of manliness. The sport was popular in the Australian colonies, particularly on the goldfields. A fight between James Kelly and Jonathan Smith on 3 December 1854 for a £400 prize at the Fiery Creek diggings in Victoria reportedly went for over six and a quarter hours. The travelling artist S.T. Gill captured many scenes of life on the Victorian goldfields, including this image of a boxing saloon in Ballarat.

DANIEL AND CHARLES HOULE (SILVERSMITHS), *Challenge Cup Heavy Weights. Presented by the Marquis [sic] of Queensberry to the Amateur Athletic Club,* 1867

THE MARQUESS OF QUEENSBERRY

Lord John Sholto Douglas, 9th Marquess of Queensberry, had an avid interest in sport. He founded the Amateur Athletic Club in London, to which this trophy was presented in 1867, and gave his name to the 'Queensberry rules' of boxing. These rules, adopted in 1866, were drawn up largely by lightweight boxing champion John Graham Chambers. They established the fundamental provisions that govern the sport today, including the use of boxing gloves, 3-minute rounds and the 10-count. The last champion recorded on the trophy is Sydney-born Sir Hubert Murray, who earned his inclusion in 1885.

PHOTOGRAPHER UNKNOWN,
Portrait of 'Professor' Billy Miller,
between 1878 and 1889

'THE PROFESSOR'

William Miller held Australian championships for wrestling, fencing, broadsword fighting, weightlifting and boxing. Known as 'the Professor', he fought New South Wales champion Larry Foley for the Australian heavyweight championship in 1883 in a hall at the Academy of Music in Castlereagh Street, Sydney. The fight went for 40 rounds and was only stopped when spectators invaded the ring. The next day, the referee and supporters of both fighters met at the Tattersall's Rooms and declared the contest a draw. In the end, however, Foley conceded he had lost to Miller; most who had seen the bout agreed.

In the 1890s, Miller managed the Melbourne Athletic Club. He later moved to the United States, where he managed the San Francisco Athletic Club and was a trainer for the New York Police Department. On his death in 1939, *The Baltimore Sun* described him as 'one of the greatest all-round athletes in the world'.

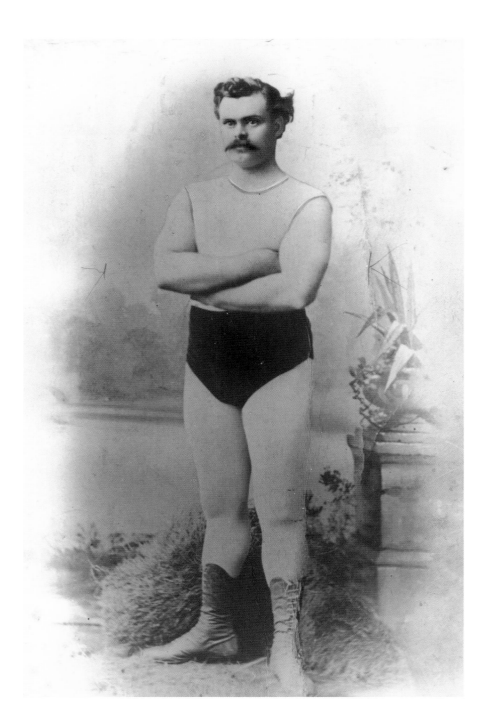

INDIGENOUS CHAMPION

Jerry Jerome was Australia's first Indigenous boxing champion. He was born at Jimbour Homestead, near Dalby in the Darling Downs, Queensland, on the traditional lands of the Yiman People. He started his career as a boxer when he was 35, much older than most fighters did. Jerome needed the permission of the Queensland Aboriginal Protection Board to compete as a professional boxer. He had more than 20 first-class fights, including notable victories over Frenchman Ercole de Balzac and British middleweight champion Jim Sullivan. On 7 September 1912 he defeated Charlie Godfrey in Brisbane, in four rounds, to claim the Middleweight Championship of Australia.

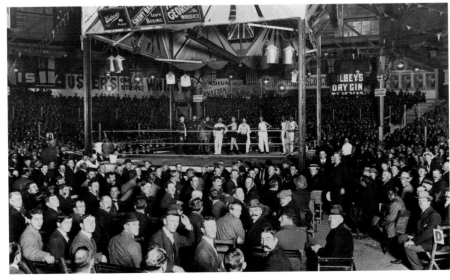

CAPTAIN. OFFICER. SUGAR. JELLICO. COUSINS. NEDDY. MULLAGH. BULLOCKY. TARPOT. SUNDOWN. PETER. UMPIRE·

PORTRAITS OF THE ABORIGINE CRICKETERS.—SEE PAGE 10.

SAMUEL CALVERT (1828–1913), *Portraits of the Aboriginal Cricketers, Victoria*, 1866

_____

AN AUSTRALIAN FIRST

The very first Australian team to tour England was an Indigenous one that originated from the cattle stations in western Victoria. After playing against the Melbourne Cricket Club before a large crowd in late 1866, financial backers enabled the team to tour England in 1868. Although *The Times* described the team as 'a travestie upon cricketing at Lord's', there was great public interest, with 20,000 spectators coming to watch the first match at The Oval. Over a six-month tour, the team performed creditably, winning 14 matches. All-rounder Johnny Mullagh starred, scoring 1,698 runs and taking 245 wickets.

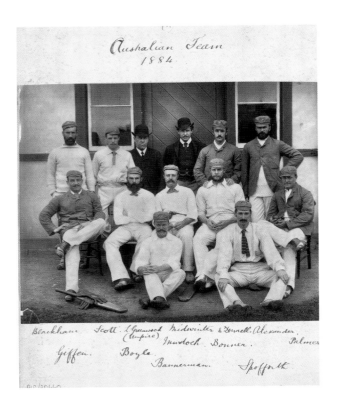

LEFT **PHOTOGRAPHER UNKNOWN,** *Group Portrait of the Australian Cricket Team,* 1884
RIGHT *England vs Australia Scorecard,* August 1882

THE BIRTH OF THE ASHES

This scorecard is from the famous 1882 Test match when Australia defeated England at home for the first time. Two days later, a mock obituary for English cricket was published in *The Sporting Times*. It concluded: 'The body will be cremated and the ashes taken to Australia'. This was the birth of the term 'the Ashes' as a name for international cricket Tests between England and Australia. When England won the subsequent series in Australia, a small urn was presented to the touring captain. Believed to contain burnt cricket bails, this urn has come to represent the legendary Ashes.

ENGLISH & AUSTRALIAN CRICKETERS
GREAT MATCH, ENGLAND v AUSTRALIA PLAYED AT LORD'S CRICKET GROUND, LONDON 19ᵗʰ 20ᵗʰ 21ˢᵗ JULY 1886.
SCORES ENGLAND 1ˢᵗ INNINGS 353 AUSTRALIANS 1ˢᵗ INNINGS 121 2ⁿᵈ INNINGS 126
ENGLAND WON BY AN INNINGS AND 106 RUNS.

I.F. WEEDON (1864–1924), *English and Australian Cricketers:*
Great Match, England vs Australia, Played at Lord's Cricket Ground,
London, 19–21 July 1886, 1887

AUSTRALIA VS ENGLAND AT LORD'S

The Australian cricket team played three Tests against England on the 1886
Ashes tour. This image depicts the second Test played at Lord's, the 'home of
cricket'. The tour was not a successful one, with the Australians losing all three
Tests. The central image is surrounded by portraits of the players, including the
legendary English player W.G. Grace, who played Test cricket into his fifties.

WILLIAM HENRY CORKHILL (1846–1936), *Tilba Tilba Ladies' Cricket Team*, c.1905

WOMEN'S CRICKET

Today Australia leads the world in women's cricket, building on a tradition of women playing the sport. What is believed to be Australia's first women's cricket match took place in 1874. Women's cricket became popular in the 1890s, when clubs emerged in different areas.

Little is known about the early twentieth-century team depicted here, from Tilba Tilba in New South Wales. The existence of this portrait indicates that the team was taken seriously in the community and that its members were supported in their participation in sport, even though some at the time considered it 'unladylike' for women to play cricket.

PHOTO No. 3

ANNETTE KELLERMANN　　　703 St. James Building
New York

PHOTOGRAPHER UNKNOWN,
*Annette Kellermann
Demonstrating Her Physical
Exercises: Photo No. 3*, c.1918

THE 'PERFECT WOMAN'
Australian Annette Kellermann
started her career as a swimmer.
In the 1900s, she was one of the
first women to attempt to swim
the English Channel, and she also
pioneered the one-piece swimsuit.
Her greatest fame, however, came
as a vaudeville performer and a
silent-era movie star, principally
in the United States. Kellermann
incorporated aquatic elements—
diving, swimming and artistic
swimming—into her performances.
Dubbed the 'Perfect Woman', owing
to her measurements, she wrote
two books touting the benefits of
exercise. This picture is from a series
that appeared in her book *Physical
Beauty: How to Keep It* (1918).

EXCHANGE STUDIOS,
Portrait of Fanny Durack, 1912

AUSTRALIA'S FIRST FEMALE OLYMPIC GOLD MEDALLIST

In 1912, Sarah 'Fanny' Durack became the first Australian woman to win Olympic gold, at the Stockholm Games. The grandeur of this portrait alludes to her success. Towel in hand, her modern one-piece swimming costume still damp, she is portrayed as an athlete. To maintain propriety, the NSW Ladies' Amateur Swimming Association had forbidden women to appear in competitions where men were present. Durack's success in various state and national competitions earned her huge public support, and it was decided that she, alongside Wilhelmina 'Mina' Wylie, could participate in Stockholm despite the ban. The pair duly finished first and second in the 100-metre freestyle.

PHOTOGRAPHER UNKNOWN, *Women and Children Playing Tennis at the Boake Family Home, North Willoughby, New South Wales*, c.1880

SOCIAL TENNIS

Tennis was introduced to Australia by the British and Americans in the late nineteenth century, around the time the modern game, using rackets and a lawn court, was established. In 1875, the first tennis court in Australia was built in Hobart, and the country's first tournament, the Championship of the Colony of Victoria, took place five years later at the Melbourne Cricket Club. As more competitions evolved, so too did community interest in the sport. Tennis was a game enjoyed socially by those with access to equipment and facilities, including women and children, as seen in this photograph.

TROEDEL & COOPER, *Enlist in the Sportsmen's 1000*, 1916

PATRIOTIC SPIRIT

In the First World War, the government used Australians' interest in sport to appeal to potential enlistees. Featuring a portrait of the first Australian to win a Victoria Cross during the war, Albert Jacka, this poster encourages young men to 'Join together, train together, embark together, fight together', suggesting that military service was akin to joining a sporting team. Other posters implied that athletes who stayed at home and continued to play sports were shirkers. Many sports suspended their competitions for the duration. Notable exceptions were the New South Wales Rugby League and the Victorian Football League, both of which continued their premiership competitions— although there were three seasons when a reduced number of clubs competed in the latter.

ARTIST UNKNOWN, *Australian Rules Football Match with Essendon Players*, c.1880

THE EARLY YEARS OF AUSTRALIAN RULES

Australian Rules is one of the earliest football codes in the world, older than rugby league, American football and even soccer. Over the years, the original rules, written by the Melbourne Football Club in 1859, have undergone significant revision. This lithograph shows goal posts without behind posts. A behind only scored a point after an update to the rules in 1897.

Many of the early Australian Rules teams still exist today. Melbourne, Geelong, Carlton, North Melbourne (originally Hotham), Port Adelaide, Essendon (pictured) and St Kilda have all retained their identities formed in the game's first two decades.

LEFT *Pioneer Exhibition Game, Australian Football*, 1916
RIGHT CECIL HARTT (1884–1930), Page 4 in *Pioneer Exhibition Game, Australian Football*, 1916

AUSTRALIAN RULES IN ENGLAND

The first Australian Rules football match played in England took place at West Kensington on 28 October 1916. It pitted the 3rd Australian Division team against the Australian Training Units Team. A special program featured cartoon sketches by some of Australia's best wartime artists, such as Cecil Hartt, Will Dyson, Ruby Lind and Fred Leist. The text provided an introduction to the rules for an English audience, describing Australian Rules as a cross between rugby and association football. 'Brilliant runs, bouncing the ball at full speed, stab-kick-passing or short, fast, low kicking to a fellow player; long kicking' were said to be the game's main features. On the day, '3rd Div' emerged victorious, 6.16 (52) to 4.12 (36).

GRASSROOTS

Supporting the local football team, going to the pool, playing tennis, golf or bowls—these are all things that Australians know well. Local teams provide entertainment for fans and help promote a sense of shared identity in villages, towns and cities. Sports carnivals and inter-school competitions help build camaraderie among students. Whether it takes the form of a school competition, a suburban sports team or an amateur tennis tournament, community sport has long been the focus of Australian sporting culture.

BRUCE HOWARD (b.1936), *Anna Bacic, Westall High School, Added 15 Feet to the Javelin Record at the Monash Division of the Metropolitan High School Sports, Melbourne,* 28 September 1972

BUILDING CHARACTER
School sports has been an enduring part of the Australian education system since the mid-nineteenth century. Early games of inter-school football were inspired by the example of British public school sport. Later, the Public Schools' Amateur Athletics Association, established in New South Wales in 1889, served to encourage school pride and *esprit de corps*. Traditionally, Australian school sport has emphasised the building of character, through the ideal of fair play, rather than merely fitness and health.

PHOTOGRAPHER UNKNOWN, *Crowds on the Hill, England vs New South Wales Football Match, Sydney Cricket Ground*, 1936

ROBIN SMITH (1927–2022), *Spectators at Australians vs The World Cricket Match Held at the Sydney Cricket Ground,* 1978

'THE HILL'

The Sydney Cricket Ground's 'Hill' was a grassed slope under the scoreboard at the southern end of the stadium. Reserved for the cheapest tickets, the Hill could be standing room only or, on less popular days, a place for picnics. It was the favourite haunt of the legendary heckler 'Yabba', who was said to scream at Douglas Jardine, the English captain during the Bodyline series, 'Leave our flies alone, Jardine. They're the only friends you've got here'.

For most of the twentieth century, the Hill remained unchanged, hosting thousands of fans for games of cricket, rugby league, rugby union and Australian Rules football. In the 1970s, it became infamous for the behaviour of fans, including heavy drinking and fighting. The Hill was demolished in 2008 and replaced by the Victor Trumper Stand.

IAN KENINS, *The Workers at the Kemcor factory in Laverton, Victoria, Have Been Lunchtime Cricketers since the mid-1970s, Come Summer and Winter,* 1996

A NATIONAL PASTIME

The rules for the improvised game known as backyard cricket, beach cricket or even garden cricket are adapted by players on the day. Sometimes a bin is used in lieu of stumps. Often there are no teams involved, and everyone takes turns to bat, bowl and field. The only essentials are a bat, a ball and a group of players with a keen interest in bowling each other out.

SERENA OVENS (b.1967), *Portrait of Nathan and Joshua Stewart,* 1993

ERN MCQUILLAN (1926–2018),
*Prince Charles at the North
Bondi Surf Club,* 1966

ERN MCQUILLAN (1926–2018),
*Queen Elizabeth II Greets
Balmain Rugby League Players
at Sydney Cricket Ground,* 1973

SPORTING ROYALS

Attending sporting events has always been a key part of royal visits. Symbolically reviewing a line of athletes is the equivalent of inspecting the best a country has to offer. The members of the team are representatives of their community and worthy of a royal handshake.

Queen Elizabeth II was famous for her passion for horseracing, but she also regularly attended Olympic events, soccer, rugby and cricket matches. King Charles III, well known as a polo player in his youth, was also interested in other sports. In 1966, while the Prince was attending Geelong Grammar School, aged 17, a special visit was organised so that he could witness the quintessential Australian sport of lifesaving at North Bondi.

The Royal Agricultural Society Challenge Shield, 1908

A NEW LEAGUE

The Royal Agricultural Society Challenge Shield was the first premiership trophy of the New South Wales Rugby League. It was awarded from 1908 to 1913, when the Agricultural Showground—the 'Ag', or 'Agra', as it was known—was the home of rugby league in Sydney. South Sydney won the shield in 1908 and 1909, Newtown in 1910 and Eastern Suburbs in 1911, 1912 and 1913. After its 1913 win, Eastern Suburbs presented the shield to its star captain, Herbert 'Dally' Messenger.

The New South Wales Rugby League was formed in 1908 as a professional breakaway code from rugby union. The new code adopted the rules of the English Northern Union, which later came to be known as rugby league.

Maher Cup, 1921

THE 'OLD TIN POT'

For many years, the Maher Cup, known as the 'Old Tin Pot', was one of the most contested rugby league prizes in New South Wales. The focus of passionate rivalry in the south of the state, the cup was awarded on a challenge basis: neighbouring towns would challenge whoever happened to hold the cup at the time. Players and supporters would arrive in a town in a blaze of glory, intent on wresting the cup from the incumbents. Originally a rugby union cup, it was first contested as a rugby league trophy in Tumut in 1921. Over the seasons, there were hundreds of challenges, involving teams such as Cootamundra, Wagga Wagga, Temora, Grenfell and many others. The cycle ended in 1971, however, when Tumut regained possession of the cup for the final time.

BARBARA MCGRADY (b.1950), *Danny Tanner with the Ball, Waterloo Storm vs Dindima, Leichhardt Oval,* 30 September–3 October 2016

THE KNOCKOUT

The NSW Koori Rugby League Knockout Carnival started as a small knockout competition in St Peters, Sydney, in 1971. In a knockout competition, teams play a series of games with only the winners proceeding to the next round. In the first year of competition there were seven teams: Koori United, Redfern All Blacks, Kempsey, La Perouse, Walgett, Moree and a combined Mount Druitt/South Coast side. The competition has now been running for over 50 years and is one of the largest football carnivals held in Australia. At the 2022 Knockout, held in the Shoalhaven district on the South Coast of New South Wales, there were over 100 teams and more than 40,000 spectators. The current champions are the Newcastle All Blacks.

Premiership Cup to Signify Geelong Football Club's 1925, 1931, 1937, 1951 and 1952 VFL Premierships

PREMIERSHIP CUP

The prestigious and hard-fought-for premiership cup is one of two awards presented to the team winning the grand final. From the very first Victorian Football League season, in 1897, premiers were awarded the premiership flag, which is traditionally unfurled at the team's first home game of the following season. From 1959, the premiership cup was awarded along with the flag. This cup was awarded to Geelong in 2004, in recognition of the club's earlier premierships.

*Painted Football Presented to Stuart Spencer, Melbourne FC,
VFL Premiers, 1956*

HAT-TRICKS AND MUCH MORE

During the 1940s and 1950s, Melbourne Football Club was a dominant force within what was then the Victorian Football League. Between 1939 and 1964, the Demons made it to 13 grand finals, winning 10 of them. This included two premiership hat-tricks (1939–1941 and 1955–1957), making them the only AFL team to have accomplished this feat.

In 1965, the team faltered. Following its success at the 1964 grand final, Melbourne lost star player Ron Barassi to Carlton, and star-player-turned-coach Norm Smith was sacked. Though Smith was quickly reinstated, Melbourne did not appear in another grand final until 1988, and did not become premiers again until 2021, 57 years after their last premiership win.

IAN KENINS, *Shirley Harris Riding Her Bowl,* 1998

LAWN BOWLS LINGO

Many sports have their own terminology. Lawn bowls is no different. Whether players are 'kissing the jack' or 'rolling a dambuster', they can all enjoy this social sport and become a part of the local club or 'bowlo'. Membership comes with the benefits of professional coaching, social events, use of facilities and members' prices at the club bar. Shirley Harris, seen here at the Albert Park Ladies Lawn Bowls Club, Victoria, would join her fellow members for an afternoon cuppa after 'riding her bowl'.

JOHN WITZIG (b.1944), *Nigel in WA,* 1972

CAPTURING THE WAVES

John Witzig co-founded *Tracks*, an iconic monthly surf magazine, in 1970. The photographer, writer and designer began taking surf photographs in the 1960s and contributing to surf magazines. With *Tracks*, he and his colleagues combined their love of surfing with broader interests, such as environmental sustainability and the arts. Together they crafted a magazine that appealed to the broad interests of the surfing community. This photograph, which appeared on the cover of the March 1972 edition, is an example of how Witzig captured the energy and beauty of surfing.

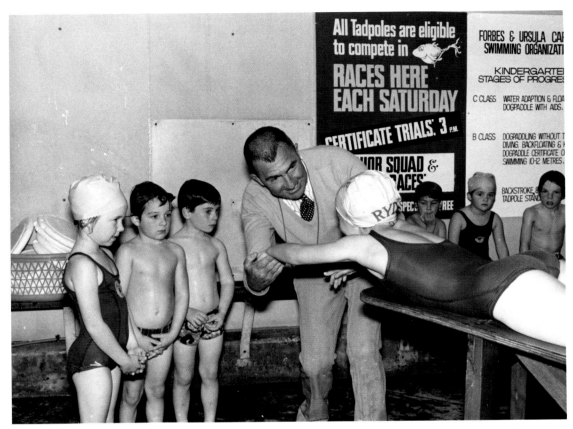

PETER KELLY, *Australian Swimming Coach Forbes Carlile Training Swimmers at Pymble Swimming School, Sydney,* 1975

LEARNING TO SWIM

Part of the reason for Australia's dominance in world swimming is the quality of its coaches. One of the most influential of these was Forbes Carlile. Working with his wife, Ursula, and their assistant, Tom Green, Carlile introduced many innovations that transformed swimming training: goggles, pace clocks, interval training, blood tests, heart rate checks and logbooks. He was also one of the pioneers of teaching children to swim in New South Wales. One of his most successful swimmers was Shane Gould, who won three gold medals, a silver and a bronze at the 1972 Munich Olympic Games. She simultaneously held world records in the 100-, 200-, 400-, 800- and 1,500-metre freestyle and in the 200-metre individual medley.

ED RADCLYFFE (b.1971), *Canberra Roller Derby League Presents CRDL Vice City Rollers vs NBR Brawl Stars in 'The Silence of the Jams': AIS Arena,* 15 December 2012

FAST AND DANGEROUS

Roller derby can trace its roots back to the United States in the 1930s. The early 2000s, however, saw a revival of the sport, which has been enthusiastically taken up by Australians. Initially, this revival was championed by women, and the early leagues were open for women players only, though men could participate in supporting roles. But men's roller derby leagues now exist. Like the women's leagues, these are administered and organised by passionate volunteers.

The sport is both highly physical and strategic. Annabelle Lecter (pictured here) of the Northern Brisbane Rollers recalls: 'as a friend once said, roller derby is like speed chess while someone throws bricks at you'.

CONOR ASHLEIGH (b.1987), *Laat Gaak, Penrith*, 2014

SHOOTING HOOPS

Laat Gaak warms up on an unused court before his team, Sydney's South Stars, plays Melbourne's Longhorns in the finals at the annual South Sudanese Summer Slam basketball competition held in Penrith, in western Sydney, in December 2014. The South Sudanese Australian National Basketball Association holds tournaments twice a year in major cities around the country. These events enable the South Sudanese community to celebrate their cultural identity. Some young Australian South Sudanese basketball players have been recruited to professional teams in the United States.

SPORTING SPECTACLES

Whether it is a football grand final, any of the many Olympic Games events or a Formula One motor race, Australians will turn out in their hundreds of thousands to watch major sporting events. The crowd numbers are matched by the ratings achieved on radio, television and streaming services. Watching sport live is a major Australian pastime. Every day, across the nation, Australians from all walks of life attend sporting events or tune in to watch their champions display their considerable skills.

FIGHT FOR THE WORLD'S CHAMPIONSHIP

TOMMY BURNS AND **JACK JOHNSON**

IN THE RING AT THE STADIUM, RUSHCUTTERS BAY, SYDNEY, N.S.W., SATURDAY, DECEMBER 26, 1908.

CHARLES KERRY (1857–1928), *Fight for the World's Championship: Tommy Burns and Jack Johnson, in the Ring at the Stadium, Rushcutters Bay, Sydney*, 26 December 1908

JOHNSON VS BURNS

One of the biggest fights in Australian boxing history did not actually feature an Australian. On Boxing Day 1908, media baron and sports entrepreneur Hugh D. McIntosh, also known as 'Huge Deal' McIntosh, staged a fight between African-American champion Jack Johnson and Canadian Tommy Burns at Rushcutters Bay, Sydney. In the racially charged climate of the times, the fight was widely reported as a clash between the black and the white races. A crowd of more than 20,000 boxing fans watched Johnson pummel Burns for 14 rounds before he was crowned first black Heavyweight Champion of the World.

CHARLES KERRY (1857–1928) *Burns–Johnson Boxing Contest, Sydney,*
26 December 1908

FILMING THE FIGHT

Hugh D. McIntosh was not satisfied with the profits he made from ticket sales
for the fight. In what would become standard practice for fight promoters,
he also organised for the fight to be filmed. In this panoramic view of the
stadium, you can clearly see a camera tower to the right of the ring. The footage
recorded that day was used to make a film, which was distributed throughout
Australia and around the world. McIntosh used the profits from the fight—and
the film—to build an octagonal roofed stadium on the Rushcutters Bay site that
could hold 12,000 people.

HERBERT H. FISHWICK (1882–1957), *Bill Woodfull Being Hit Out by Harold Larwood during the Third Test Cricket Match, Adelaide,* 1933

BODYLINE

The 1932–1933 Ashes series is the most famous of all time. To counter Donald Bradman's legendary batting in the 1930 series, England came up with a strategy known as 'leg theory'. The ball was bowled short into the batter's body, forcing him to use his bat to protect himself. Fielders were placed in close to catch any deflections. England won the series 4–1, but their unsporting tactics caused popular outrage. The crowd nearly rioted in the Adelaide Test when Australian captain Bill Woodfull was hit over the heart and wicketkeeper Bert Oldfield had his skull fractured.

ABOVE: PHOTOGRAPHER UNKNOWN,
*Hazel Pritchard (NSW) with Doris Turner
and Betty Snowball (England), Sydney,* 1935
RIGHT: M. JEGUST, *Souvenir Program for World's
First International Women's Cricket Match,* 1934

THE FIRST WOMEN'S INTERNATIONAL CRICKET TOUR

The first ever women's Tests occurred in 1934–1935, when England toured Australia. Three Ashes Tests were played in Brisbane, Sydney and Melbourne, as well as games against state sides. England won the Test series 2–0. Myrtle Maclagan starred for the tourists, with 26 wickets for the series. While there was none of the acrimony of the earlier men's Bodyline series, Australian wicketkeeper Hilda Hills had her nose broken in the first Test.

CHARLES MEERE (1890–1961),
*Empire Games: Sydney Calls
You ...*, 1938

CELEBRATING EMPIRE
Coinciding with celebrations of
Australia's 150th anniversary in
1938, the British Empire Games
were held over the week 5–12
February in Sydney. Fifteen
countries were represented by
466 athletes who competed in track
and field events, swimming and
diving, lawn bowls, cycling, boxing,
wrestling and rowing. Australia was
the most successful competing
nation, finishing with a total of
66 medals. Sprinter Decima Norman
from Albany, Western Australia,
provided the nation with five of its
six track and field gold medals.
The British Empire Games, which
began in 1930, were renamed the
Commonwealth Games in 1978.

MAX FORBES (1923–1990),
*Melbourne, Olympic City,
Australia,* 1956

A SOUTHERN OLYMPICS

The first Olympic Games to be staged in the Southern Hemisphere were the 1956 Summer Olympics, or Games of the XVI Olympiad. They were held from 22 November to 8 December 1956 in Melbourne, with the exception of the equestrian events, which had been held in Sweden in June 1956.

While the Soviet Union won the most medals overall, Australian athletes were very successful. Betty Cuthbert won the 100- and 200-metre sprint races, and Shirley Strickland won gold in the 80-metre hurdles. They were both a part of the winning 4 x 100-metre relay team. Australians, including Murray Rose and Dawn Fraser, won all of the freestyle swimming races.

Letter from John Ian Wing to the Melbourne Olympic Games
Committee, 1956

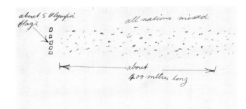

'PARADE OF ATHLETES'

War, politics and nationality will be all forgotten, what more could anybody want, if the whole world could be made as one nation?

Seven countries boycotted the 1956 Melbourne Olympic Games owing to various international tensions. Violence broke out at a water polo match between the Soviet Union and Hungarian teams. John Ian Wing, a 17-year-old Chinese-Australian apprentice carpenter, wanted the closing ceremony to symbolise global unity. A few days before the ceremony, he wrote to the organising committee suggesting that athletes walk in together, rather than in their national teams, and wave to the spectators. The 'Parade of Athletes' has continued to be a part of closing ceremonies since 1956.

BRUCE HOWARD (b.1936),
*Olympic Athletes March
Together during the Closing
Ceremony of the Melbourne
Olympics, Melbourne Cricket
Ground,* 1956

State of Origin Shield, 1980

MATE AGAINST MATE, STATE AGAINST STATE

For many Australian rugby league fans, the most significant trophy of all is the first State of Origin Shield. The birth of State of Origin football in 1980 ushered in a new era of rugby league history. After years of New South Wales dominating Queensland, new life was injected into interstate football when, as an experiment in the third match of the 1980 series, it was decided that players would represent their state of origin, rather than the state where they happened to be playing at the time. The result was a sensational Queensland victory, and interstate football has since become the pinnacle of the game.

This trophy, sponsored by Winfield, was awarded in competition 'for rugby league supremacy between New South Wales and Queensland' from 1980 to 1991. It depicts two legends of the game, Brett Kenny (New South Wales) and Wally Lewis (Queensland), locked in a fierce arm wrestle.

MAKING MONEY

Tobacco, beer and poker machines—sport has a long history of being used to sell things. Sporting entrepreneurs know that fans will pay to see their champions. Gambling, admission tickets, memberships, media, advertising, endorsements and sponsorship all provide ways to generate income from sporting spectacles. These forces have seen elite Australian sport slowly shift from a proud amateur tradition to an increasingly commercial focus. This move to professionalism was resisted by some sports bodies, such as the Olympic movement and rugby union, but by the end of the twentieth century the best athletes had embraced being paid to play. It was only fair that athletes needing to train full-time should be paid for their hard work and compensated for the possibility of injury.

S.T. LEIGH & CO (PRINTERS),
Capstan Test Cricket Calendar,
1949 (Featuring Don Bradman),
1948

SELLING SMOKES

In the early twentieth century
Capstan was one of the most popular
brands of cigarettes in Australia.
The company's advertising strategy
included producing collectable
items, such as cigarette cards and
calendars featuring images of
famous cricketers and footballers.
This example celebrates one of
Australia's greatest cricket teams of
all time, the 1948 Australian touring
side to England. Led by Donald
Bradman, the team completed
the tour undefeated, earning the
nickname 'the Invincibles'.

While restrictions on cigarette
advertising were introduced in the
1970s, tobacco promotion continued
through sponsorship of sports such
as cricket, motor racing and football.
Tobacco sponsorship was eventually
banned in Australia in 1992.

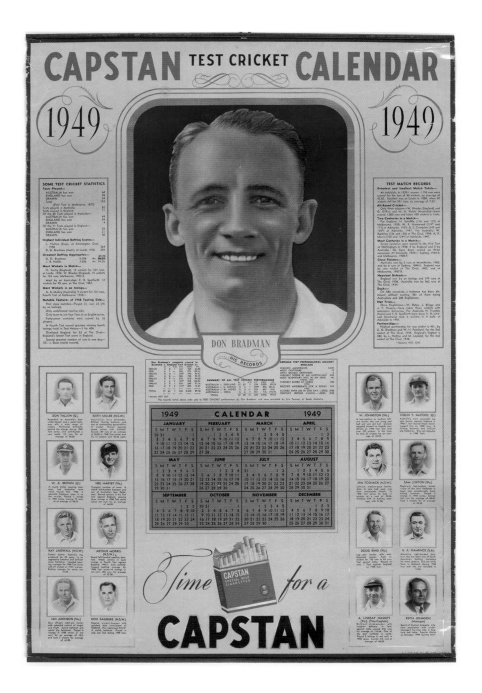

'Breathe Easy': Toohey's 2.2
Lite Lager Beer , c.1985

BEER AND SPORT

Beer advertising has had a long relationship with sport, with various brews over the years being spruiked by boxers, cricketers and footballers. Australian cricketers Doug Walters and Max Walker promoted moderation in drinking with their endorsement of Toohey's 2.2 low-alcohol brand in the 1980s.

Walters had an impressive record as a batter, including hitting centuries in his first two Test innings in 1965, and another in a session against England in the 1974 Test at the Western Australian Cricket Ground. He also held an unofficial record for the most cans of beer consumed on a flight from Australia to England. His 44-can record was later bested by Rod Marsh, who downed 45, and then by David Boon, with 51 to his credit. No recent Australian cricketer has attempted to break the record.

PHOTOGRAPHER UNKNOWN, *West End Bitter Beer Advertisement Featuring Boxing Identities, South Australia*, c.1910

GERRY WEDD (b.1957), *Mambo Tapestry of Surfing History,* 1995

SELLING A LIFESTYLE

Born out of necessity, surf fashion has become a large part of the casual fashion market. Initially small businesses run out of homes, surfing brands have grown to offer a whole range of clothing and accessories sold in stores worldwide, even those far from the ocean. They later branched out to include all manner of board sports, such as skateboarding, skiing and snowboarding.

Founded by Dare Jennings and Andrew Rich in 1984, Mambo used the work of established artists to introduce art and humour to the industry. It was a polarising brand, embraced by Australia's youth but seen as controversial by more conservative consumers.

Malvern Star: The Cycle of Opperman, 1934

'FAMED THE WORLD OVER'

For much of the twentieth century one name was synonymous with Australian cycling: Hubert Opperman. Opperman gained international renown in 1928, when he captained the first Australasian team to enter the Tour de France, finishing 18th out of 262 riders. Six weeks later, he competed in the gruelling Bol d'Or, a 24-hour velodrome race. Despite sabotage to both his bikes, he rode 53 kilometres further than his opponents, then pushed on alone for an extra 79 minutes to break the world record for 1,000 kilometres. Opperman's sponsorship by Malvern Star bicycles made both household names. He resisted enticing overtures from commercial competitors, remaining loyal to the brand and its owner, his lifelong friend Bruce Small.

TOWARDS A LEVEL PLAYING FIELD

The professionalisation of elite women's sport, while occurring later than for men, has gathered momentum in recent decades. Golf and tennis tournaments saw an increase in prize money for women in the 1970s, though it was still modest in comparison to the men's prizes. Women's basketball established a national league in Australia in the 1980s, putting it on a path towards becoming fully professional. More recently, professional women's national leagues have been established in soccer (2008), cricket (2015), netball (2016), Australian Rules football (2017) and rugby league (2018). These sports have also negotiated broadcast and sponsorship agreements that brought more money into their codes. While the pay gap has not fully closed, elite women's sport has been transformed.

MARK METCALFE, *The Capitals Celebrate Victory during the Round 10 WNBL Match between UC Capitals and Bendigo Spirit at the National Convention Centre,* 11 January 2023

A DOMINANT TEAM

The University of Canberra Capitals are a dominant team in Australia's Women's National Basketball League (WNBL). The team, previously known as the Canberra Capitals, was founded in 1984 and made its debut in the WNBL two years later. The Capitals' dominance began in 1999, led by two legends of the game, coach Carrie Graf and player Lauren Jackson. Since then, they have won nine WNBL championships, the most recent being the 2019–2020 season.

QUINN ROONEY, *The Victorious Australian Women's Cricket Team,* 2020

THE GREATEST TEAM EVER?

The Australian men's cricket team has the most successful record across the One-Day and Twenty20 formats with six World Cup trophies. In comparison, the Australian women's team has won an incredible 13 World Cups across both formats. In 2020, on International Women's Day, they lifted the Twenty20 trophy in front of 86,000 fans at the Melbourne Cricket Ground.

HANNAH PETERS, *Australian Captain Meg Lanning Celebrates Winning the 2022 One-Day World Cup*, 2022

DYLAN BURNS, *Lauren Pearce of the Demons and Caitlin Gould of the Crows Compete for the Ball during the 2022 AFLW Grand Final Match between the Adelaide Crows and the Melbourne Demons at Adelaide Oval,* 9 April 2022

AFLW: WORTH THE WAIT

2017 marked the inaugural season of AFL Women's, Australia's much anticipated national women's football league. The competition started with 8 teams, and rapidly expanded to 18. The Adelaide Crows have quickly become a powerhouse in the AFLW. They hold the distinction of having won the first grand final, in 2017, and also the most grand finals, with follow-up successes in 2019 and 2022.

Despite having only recently been professionalised, women's Australian Rules football has a history dating back over a century. Patriotic fundraising matches are documented from 1917, but there are also unverified reports of scratch matches dating back to 1886.

CHRIS MCGRATH, *The TAB Sydney Swifts Celebrate Victory in the Commonwealth Bank Trophy Netball Grand Final between the Sydney Swifts and the Adelaide Thunderbirds,* 2001

ALL PLAY, NO PAY

Netball was classed as an amateur sport between 1997 and 2007. The Commonwealth Bank Trophy (aka National Netball League) had eight teams playing at an elite level. Ineligible to be paid as professional athletes, the players were given grants of $2,040 to cover their time off work and training expenses. Match payments were not permitted, and all related earnings had to be paid into a trust fund. Sydney Swifts Captain Liz Ellis completed a law degree and was admitted to the bar—all while playing a record 173 games. To this day, netball remains the number one participation sport for Australian girls.

SUPERSTARS

Sporting heroes are elevated beyond everyday life. Names such as Don Bradman and Shane Warne, or Cathy Freeman and Ash Barty, have come to conjure up much more than simply individual examples of sporting greatness. They have become part of the social glue that draws Australians together. These sporting superstars help build a sense of community and pride, not only on the local or national level, but also on the world stage.

DAVID MOORE (1927–2003),
*Portrait of Dawn Fraser,
Melbourne,* 1963

SWIMMING LEGEND

In 1993, Dawn Fraser became the
first female member of the Sport
Australia Hall of Fame to be elevated
to Legend of Australian Sport. A
popular swimmer, Fraser was the
first woman and first swimmer to
win the same event, the 100-metre
freestyle, across three Olympic
Games (1956, 1960 and 1964).
She was banned from competitive
swimming by the Australian
Swimming Union following a
controversial incident in Japan
during the 1964 Olympics. Although
the ban was later lifted, it was not
done in time for her to compete at
the 1968 Olympics and led to her
retirement from swimming.

PHOTOGRAPHER UNKNOWN,
Portrait of Don Bradman,
c.1930s

THE DON

More than two decades after his death, Sir Donald Bradman remains Australia's best-known sports personality. Statistically, his batting achievements on the international cricket stage show him to be 40 per cent better than other greats, such as Steve Smith. He still holds the record for most runs scored in a series: 974 in the 1930 Ashes tour of England. In that series, he famously scored 309 in a single day in the Headingley Test. In his final innings in 1948, needing to score just four runs to finish with a career average of 100 runs an innings, Bradman was stunningly dismissed for nought.

STEVE HOLLAND (b.1963),
*Australian Cricketer Shane
Warne at the End of the Fourth
Test of the Ashes Series,
Melbourne Cricket Ground*, 2006

THE SHOWMAN RETIRES

Shane Warne is widely regarded as the greatest spin bowler Australia has ever produced. His playing style combined skill, showmanship, intimidation and a sheer will to win. Controversies prevented him being made permanent Australian captain: he was banned for one year for taking a proscribed drug and fined for taking money from an illegal bookmaker. Warne was named player of the match in his penultimate Test before his home fans at the Melbourne Cricket Ground in 2006. After he died in 2022, he was honoured with a state funeral and a stand at the ground was named after him.

ALEX DAVIDSON, *Steve Smith Celebrates Double Century,* 2019

REDEMPTION

During a Test match in South Africa in 2018, members of the Australian men's cricket team were caught using sandpaper to tamper with the ball in an attempt to gain an unfair advantage. For his part in this episode, Steve Smith was stripped of the captaincy and banned for one year. He returned to the team for the 2019 Ashes series against England. Despite missing a match with concussion, he plundered 774 runs in the series. The highlight was a double century in the fourth Test. Largely due to his performances, Australia retained the Ashes in England for the first time since 2001.

MICHAEL STEELE, *Cadel Evans, Yellow Jersey Wearer of Team BMC Turns the Corner at L'Arc De Triomphe during the Twenty-First and Final Stage of Le Tour de France 2011*

TAKING THE YELLOW JERSEY

The Tour de France is widely regarded as the world's most prestigious bicycle race. The gruelling three-week race covers about 3,500 kilometres, and the winner is awarded the yellow jersey for the lowest combined time for all 21 stages.

In 2011, Cadel Evans raced in a career-defining sixth Tour de France. Having fractured his elbow during the previous year's race, and then lost his coach, Aldo Sassi, to cancer in December of 2010, his path had been far from painless. Despite these hardships, Evans began the race strongly, and came second in the individual time trial, the penultimate stage. This placed him first in the overall standing, and secured the yellow jersey. Evans remains the only Australian to have won the Tour de France.

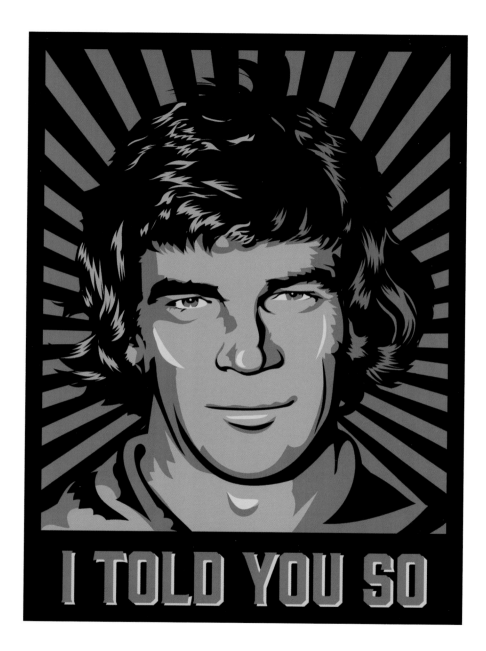

I TOLD YOU SO

ROB MORRISON, *I Told You So*

THE TRUE BELIEVER
Johnny Warren was a passionate advocate for Australian soccer. He captained the Socceroos and played in the 1974 World Cup finals when Australia qualified for the first time. After retirement, he became a soccer broadcaster. Before he died in 2004, he was asked what he would like his legacy to be. 'I told you so', he answered, in reference to the continued rise of soccer in Australia. A year after his death, Australia qualified for the World Cup for a second time. They have qualified for every World Cup finals tournament since.

ADAM PETTY, *John Aloisi Kicks the Winning Penalty to Qualify Australia for the 2006 World Cup*, 2005

TONY FEDER, *Kerr's Trademark Backflip,* 2017

THE GOLDEN BOOT

Australian soccer captain Sam Kerr is undisputedly the greatest Australian player of all time. She holds the record for the most goals scored in the US professional league. Kerr has also won the golden boot award for most goals in a season in the English Women's Super League twice. In 2019, she became the first Australian player to score a hat-trick at a World Cup. Kerr's playing style is more effective than flashy. She has a poacher's instinct, with an uncanny ability to position herself to win the ball and score. Her trademark goal celebration is a running cartwheel into a backflip.

BRUCE HOWARD (b.1936),
Sydney's Warwick Capper
Taking a Spectacular Mark over
Mick Martin of the Kangaroos
in a Game at the MCG on Anzac
Day, 1991

THE HIGH MARK

What a spectacular leap! ...
Watch the big men fly! ...
Jesaulenko, you beauty!

The 'specky'. The 'screamer'.
Spectacular marks are one of
the most celebrated hallmarks
of Australian Rules football.
The moment a player leaps high
over an opponent to pluck the ball
out of the air can become cemented
in football legend. The player, falling
back to earth, has been likened by
poet Bruce Dawe to a 'guernseyed
Icarus'.

SERENA OVENS (b.1967),
*Portrait of Louise Sauvage OAM,
Atlanta, Georgia, USA,* 1996

RACING FROM THE FRONT

*I was stuffed at the end of it—but
happy. I had four gold medals, 400,
800, 1,500 and 5,000 metres, plus
the one from the Olympic Games,
and was just so glad it was all over.*

Louise Sauvage achieved
two world records at the Atlanta
Paralympic Games in 1996. Since
retiring from competition after the
2004 Athens Paralympic Games,
she has coached young wheelchair
athletes. In 2001, she established
a foundation to support athletes
with disabilities. And, in 2019, she
became the first para-athlete to be
honoured as the 41st Legend of
Australian Sport.

CHRISTIAN PETERSEN, *Lauren Jackson #15 of Australia Celebrates in the Second Half against Russia during the Women's Basketball Bronze Medal Game on Day 15 of the London 2012 Olympic Games,* 11 August 2012

A BASKETBALL LEGEND

Lauren Jackson ranks among the greatest basketball players of all time. Her career highlights with the Opals, the Australian national women's basketball team, include four Olympic medals, four World Cup medals (including one gold) and a Commonwealth Games gold medal. She was drafted in the US Women's National Basketball Association (WNBA) league in 2001, picked as a 'franchise player' by the Seattle Storm, and won many accolades. She made a significant impact in Australia's WNBL, playing for teams such as the Canberra Capitals (now the University of Canberra Capitals). She was inducted into the Women's Basketball Hall of Fame in 2020.

THOMAS COEX, *Australia's Patty Mills Goes to the Basket in the Men's Bronze Medal Basketball Match between Slovenia and Australia during the Tokyo 2020 Olympic Games,* 7 August 2021

CLINCHING A LONG-AWAITED OLYMPIC MEDAL

Patrick 'Patty' Mills, a Muralag Torres Strait Islander and Kokatha Aboriginal man, led Australia's men's national basketball team to their first Olympic medal in 2021. He scored a game high of 42 points when the Boomers beat Slovenia to claim bronze at the Tokyo 2020 Olympic Games. This was a breakthrough for men's basketball in Australia. The team's previous best results had been fourth at the Seoul, Atlanta, Sydney and Rio de Janeiro Games. Mills, who was raised in Canberra, currently plays for the Brooklyn Nets in the prestigious North American NBA league.

CLIVE BRUNSKILL, *Anna Meares of Australia Celebrates Winning the Gold Medal in the Women's Sprint Track Cycling Final on Day 11 of the London 2012 Olympic Games at the Velodrome, London,* 7 August 2012

COMEBACK AFTER A FALL

Anna Meares has one of Australia's most remarkable comeback stories. Having won gold and set a world record for the women's 500-metre time trial at the 2004 Athens Olympic Games, Meares was set to make a strong showing at the 2008 Games. But just seven months before the Beijing Olympics, she was involved in a racing fall that fractured her C2 vertebra.

Despite the injury, which had threatened to paralyse or even kill her, Meares resumed training just 10 days later. Through an intensive rehabilitation program—and astonishing conviction—Meares won a women's sprint silver medal in 2008. However, she was not satisfied and redoubled her efforts. At the 2012 London Olympics, Meares took home the gold medal for the women's sprint, using a tactic specifically developed to defeat arch-rival Victoria Pendleton.

ELSA GARRISON, *Dylan Alcott of Australia Celebrates with the Championship Trophy after Defeating Niels Vink of the Netherlands to Complete a 'Golden Slam' during Their Wheelchair Quad Singles Final Match on Day 14 of the 2021 US Open*, 12 September 2021

THE GOLDEN SLAM

Completing a golden slam is no mean feat. It involves winning all four major tennis titles (Australian Open, French Open, Wimbledon and US Open) plus an Olympic, Paralympic or Youth Olympic gold medal in a calendar year. In 2021, Australian wheelchair tennis player Dylan Alcott became the first Australian to achieve the feat. A multi-talented athlete, he earned his first Paralympic gold medal in 2008 with the Australian men's national wheelchair basketball team, the Rollers. Alcott was named Australian of the Year in 2022, for his sporting achievements and his advocacy for people with a disability.

JARED C. TILTON, *Minjee Lee of Australia Plays a Shot from the Bunker near the 14th Green during the Final Round of the 77th U.S. Women's Open*, 2022

A DETERMINED GOLFER

Minjee Lee has come a long way since learning to play golf at age 10. Lee began her professional career in 2014, having previously ranked number one on the amateur circuit. In 2022, she became one of only three Australian women ever to win the US Women's Open, with a score of 271—the lowest 72-hole winning score in US women's history. Lee's next goal is to become the first Australian woman to achieve a world number one ranking.

TIM CLAYTON, *Gold Medal Winner Emma McKeon of Australia after the Women's 50-metre Freestyle Final at the Tokyo Aquatic Centre during the Tokyo 2020 Olympic Games,* 1 August 2021

AUSTRALIA'S MOST DECORATED OLYMPIAN

Few could have predicted what Emma McKeon would achieve at the 2020 Tokyo Olympic Games (which were actually staged in 2021, owing to the COVID-19 pandemic). She earned seven medals in Tokyo (four gold and three bronze), equalling the record of the greatest number of Olympic medals won by a woman at a single Games. In Tokyo, she was the most decorated Olympian in any sport. With 11 Olympic medals, McKeon is Australia's most decorated Olympian of all time. All eyes are on McKeon to see if she will smash more records at the upcoming 2024 Olympic Games in Paris.

IMAGE CREDITS

All items are from the collections of the National Library of Australia, unless otherwise indicated.

**front cover
(clockwise from top left)**
See page 8; see page 76; see page 85

**back cover
(clockwise from top left)**
See page 41; see page 2; see page 74

2
William Henry Corkhill (1846–1936)
Tilba Tilba Ladies' Cricket Team c.1905
glass negative
William Henry Corkhill Tilba Tilba Photograph Collection
nla.cat-vn2022916

5
S.T. Gill (1818–1880)
McLaren's Boxing Saloon, Main Road, Ballarat 1854
watercolour, 26.3 x 36.5cm
Rex Nan Kivell Collection
nla.cat-vn456864

7
I.F. Weedon (1864–1924)
English and Australian Cricketers Great Match, England vs Australia Played at Lord's Cricket Ground, London, 19–21 July 1886
London: John Harrop, 1887
hand col. lithograph, 63.2 x 85cm
Rex Nan Kivell Collection
nla.cat-vn2280835

8
David Moore (1927–2003)
Portrait of Dawn Fraser, Melbourne 1963
photograph, 39 x 26.4cm
Portraits of Notable Australians
nla.cat-vn3573345

10
Photographer unknown
Group Portrait of the Australian Cricket Team 1884
albumen print, 19.3 x 24.5cm
nla.cat-vn7578631

11
Edward Roper (1832–1909)
A Kangaroo Hunt under Mount Zero, the Grampians, Victoria, Australia 1880
oil on canvas, 79.8 x 110cm
Rex Nan Kivell Collection
nla.cat-vn1844414

12
Walter G. Mason (1820–1866)
The Flying Pieman, a Celebrated Sydney Pedestrian
Sydney: J.R. Clarke, 1807
wood engraving, 13.6 x 10.3cm
Rex Nan Kivell Collection
nla.cat-vn2660061

13
Artist unknown
The Pedestrian Wonder and Champion of the World
London: George Newbold, 1866
col. lithograph, 47.5 x 32.2cm
Rex Nan Kivell Collection
nla.cat-vn2623472

14
Adam Lindsay Gordon (1833–1870)

Mount Gambier Grand National c.1861
pen and ink, 18.1 x 30.3cm
nla.cat-vn2676520

15
J. Ryan
Flemington Racecourse from the Footscray Side of Salt Water River, Victoria c.1845
oil on canvas, 65.2 x 90.7cm
Rex Nan Kivell Collection
nla.cat-vn313470

16
Batchelder & Co.
The First Melbourne Cup Trophy 1865
photograph
nla.cat-vn5039757

17
Charles H. Kerry (1857–1928)
Miss Yan Ski Jumping, Snowy Mountains, New South Wales
Sydney: Australian Consolidated Press, c.1900
photograph
Tyrrell Collection
nla.cat-vn5080727

18
Eugene Montagu 'Monty' Scott (illustrator, 1835–1909); Gibbs, Shallard & Co. (printers and lithographers)
Sculling Match on the Thames, June 27 1876, Joseph Henry Sadler, Champion of the World, Versus Edward Trickett, of New South Wales
Sydney: *Illustrated Sydney News*, August 1876
lithograph, 52 x 72cm
nla.cat-vn2623415

19
Artist unknown
Sculling Race on River, Dent Royal Hotel c.1870
oil on canvas, 108.9 x 149.4cm
nla.cat-vn1856761

20
See page 5

21
Daniel and Charles Houle (silversmiths, active 1843–1884)
Challenge Cup Heavy Weights. Presented by the Marquis [sic] of Queensberry to the Amateur Athletic Club 1867
silver, 36.5 x 24.9 x 18cm
nla.cat-vn384095

22
Photographer unknown
Portrait of 'Professor' Billy Miller between 1878 and 1889
photograph, 30.7 x 25.5cm
Arnold Thomas Boxing Collection
nla.cat-vn3258658

23 (top)
Photographer unknown
Portrait of Jerry Jerome c.1912
photograph, 17.9 x 12.8cm
Arnold Thomas Boxing Collection
nla.cat-vn3772764

23 (bottom)
Photographer unknown
Dave Smith vs Jerry Jerome, Sydney Stadium 19 April 1913
photograph, 19 x 29.7cm
Arnold Thomas Boxing Collection
nla.cat-vn3260495

24
Samuel Calvert (1828–1913)
*Portraits of the Aboriginal
Cricketers, Victoria*
Melbourne: Ebenezer and
David Syme, 1866
engraving, 49.4 x 15cm
nla.cat-vn1177220

25 (left) See page 10

25 (right)
England vs Australia Scorecard
[England]: Surrey County
Cricket Club, 1882
15.6 x 11.8cm
nla.cat-vn64515

26 See page 7

27 See page 2

28
Photographer unknown
*Annette Kellermann
Demonstrating Her Physical
Exercises: Photo No.3* c.1918
photograph, 17.1 x 10.5cm
nla.cat-vn3044533

29
Exchange Studios
Portrait of Fanny Durack 1912
photograph, 139 x 83.5cm
nla.cat-vn89140

30
Photographer unknown
*Women and Children Playing
Tennis at the Boake Family
Home, North Willoughby, New
South Wales* c.1880
albumen print, 15.1 x 20.4cm
Views of Sydney, New South
Wales
nla.cat-vn7219699

31
Troedel & Cooper
Enlist in the Sportsmen's 1000
Melbourne: Parliamentary

Recruiting Committee, 1916
col. poster, 101 x 76.4cm
nla.cat-vn4218752

32
*Australian Rules Football
Match with Essendon Players*
c.1880
chromolithograph, 13.7 x
12.5cm
nla.cat-vn8810105

33
*Pioneer Exhibition Game,
Australian Football*
London: Australian
Commonwealth Military
Forces, 1916
25 x 15.4cm
Australian Ephemera
Collection
nla.cat-vn4192692

34
Serena Ovens (b.1967)
*Portrait of Nathan and Joshua
Stewart* 1993
gelatin silver, 21.8 x 20.4cm
nla.cat-vn2840906

35
Bruce Howard (b.1936)
*Anna Bacic, Westall High
School, Added 15 Feet to
the Javelin Record at the
Monash Division of the
Metropolitan High School
Sports, Melbourne, Victoria* 28
September 1972
b&w photograph, 15.2 x
20.5cm
Nostalgic Look at Australian
Sport Photograph Collection
nla.cat-vn6814456

36
Photographer unknown
*Crowds on the Hill, England
vs New South Wales Football
Match, Sydney Cricket Ground*
1936

*Newcastle Morning Herald
and Miners' Advocate* Archive,
1900–1960
nla.cat-vn7887634

37
Robin Smith (1927–2022)
*Spectators at Australians vs
The World Cricket Match Held
at the Sydney Cricket Ground*
1978
digital photograph
nla.cat-vn5972805

38
Ian Kenins
*The Workers at the Kemcor
factory in Laverton, Victoria,
Have Been Lunchtime
Cricketers since the mid-1970s,
Come Summer and Winter*
1996
transparency
Domestic Cricket: A Very
Australian Obsession
nla.cat-vn2476800

39 See page 34

40
Ern McQuillan (1926–2018)
*Prince Charles at the North
Bondi Surf Club, with Club
President Charlie Christenson*
1966
b&w photograph; 19.4 x
24.3cm
nla.cat-vn3562116

41
Ern McQuillan (1926–2018)
*Queen Elizabeth II Greets
Balmain Rugby League Players
at Sydney Cricket Ground* 1973
digital photograph
nla.cat-vn4493029

42
*The Royal Agricultural Society
Challenge Shield Presented to
Herbert 'Daily' Messenger by*

*the Eastern Suburbs District
Rugby Football Club with
Hanging Chain* 1908
realia, 75.5 x 63.5 x 6cm
Courtesy National Museum of
Australia
2005.0024.0001

43
Maher Cup 1921
silverplate, 43 x 23 x 21cm
Photograph courtesy National
Museum of Australia
Loan courtesy Tumut Rugby
League Old Boys Inc.

44
Barbara McGrady (b.1950)
*Danny Tanner with the
Ball, Waterloo Storm vs
Dindima, Leichhardt Oval* 30
September–3 October 2016
digital photograph
Mitchell Library, State Library
of New South Wales
Courtesy Barbara McGrady

45
*Premiership Cup to Signify
Geelong Football Club's 1925,
1931, 1937, 1951 and 1952 VFL
Premierships*
Courtesy Geelong Football
Club

46
*Painted Football Presented to
Stuart Spencer, Melbourne FC,
VFL Premiers* 1956
Kindly donated by Stuart
Spencer to the Melbourne
Cricket Club Museum
Courtesy Melbourne Cricket
Club, M4845

47
Ian Kenins
Shirley Harris Riding Her Bowl
1998
b&w photograph, 22.6 x
15.3cm

Albert Park Ladies Lawn Bowls Club, Melbourne
nla.cat-vn1739915

48
John Witzig (b.1944)
Nigel in WA 1972
photograph, 40 x 60cm
Surfing in Australia and Hawaii, 1969–1976
nla.cat-vn8812372

49
Peter Kelly
Australian Swimming Coach Forbes Carlile Training Swimmers at Pymble Swimming School, Sydney 1975
b&w photograph, 15.5 x 20.3cm
nla.cat-vn4365117

50
Ed Radclyffe (b.1971)
Canberra Roller Derby League Presents CRDL Vice City Rollers vs NBR Brawl Stars in 'The Silence of the Jams': AIS Arena 15 December 2012
illustrated poster, 84.1 x 29.7cm
nla.cat-vn6252288

51
Conor Ashleigh (b.1987)
Laat Gaak Warms up on Court before His Team, the Sydney's South Stars Play Melbourne's Longhorns in the Finals, Sydney 2014
digital photograph
Australia's South Sudanese Refugee Community, 2010–2015
nla.cat-vn7459994

52
Bruce Howard (b.1936)
Olympic Athletes March Together during the Closing Ceremony of the Melbourne Olympics, Melbourne Cricket Ground 1956
photograph, 20.2 x 25.4cm
Olympic Games, Melbourne, Victoria, 1956
Donated by Bruce Howard through the Australian Government's Cultural Gifts Program, 2007
nla.cat-vn4368569

53
Charles Kerry (1857–1928)
Fight for the World's Championship: Tommy Burns and Jack Johnson, in the Ring at the Stadium, Rushcutters Bay, Sydney 26 December 1908
poster, 26.2 x 37cm
Arnold Thomas Boxing Collection
nla.cat-vn3638997

54
Charles Kerry (1857–1928)
Burns–Johnson Boxing Contest, Sydney 26 December 1908
photograph, 37.2 x 94.8cm
nla.cat-vn3060336

55
Herbert H. Fishwick (1882–1957)
Bill Woodfull Being Hit Out by Harold Larwood during the Third Test Cricket Match, Adelaide 1933
glass negative
nla.cat-vn6304213

56 (top)
Photographer unknown
Hazel Pritchard (NSW) with Doris Turner and Betty Snowball (England), Sydney 1935
gelatin silver
Women's Cricket Association Tour of Australia, 1934–1935
nla.cat-vn3255993

56 (bottom)
M. Jegust
Souvenir Program for World's First International Women's Cricket Match
Perth: West Australian Women's Cricket Assoc., 1934
nla.cat-vn574779

57
Charles Meere (1890–1961)
Empire Games: Sydney Calls You …
Sydney: 1938
poster, 101.7 x 63.9cm
nla.cat-vn6186739

58
Max Forbes (1923–1990)
Melbourne, Olympic City, Capital of Victoria, Australia
Melbourne: 1956
poster, 120 x 82cm
nla.cat-vn2258482

59
John Ian Wing
Letter from John Ian Wing to the Melbourne Olympic Games Committee 1956
Papers of Sir Wilfred Selwyn Kent Hughes, 1914–1986
nla.cat-vn2631927

60 See page 52

61
State of Origin Shield 1980
realia, 60 x 55 x 4cm
Photograph courtesy National Museum of Australia
Loan courtesy National Rugby League

62
'Breathe Easy': Toohey's 2.2 Lite Lager Beer
Sydney: Tooheys, between 1982 and 1990
poster, 60.2 x 40cm
nla.cat-vn7012892

63
S.T. Leigh & Co (printers)
Capstan Test Cricket Calendar, 1949 (Featuring Don Bradman)
Sydney: Capstan, c.1948
broadside, 74 x 49cm
nla.cat-vn2943388

64 See page 62

65
Photographer unknown
West End Bitter Beer Advertisement Featuring Boxing Identities, South Australia c.1910
photograph, 24 x 27.9cm
Arnold Thomas Boxing Collection
nla.cat-vn3259169

66
Gerry Wedd (b.1957)
Mambo Tapestry of Surfing History
Sydney: Mambo Graphics PL, 1995
poster, 99 x 69cm
nla.cat-vn6617137

67
Malvern Star: The Cycle of Opperman
Sydney: 1934
poster, 72 x 48cm
nla.cat-vn3534118

68
Chris McGrath
The TAB Sydney Swifts Celebrate Victory in the Commonwealth Bank Trophy Netball Grand Final between the Sydney Swifts and the Adelaide Thunderbirds 2001
Getty Images

69
Mark Metcalfe
The Capitals Celebrate Victory during the Round 10 WNBL

Match between UC Capitals and Bendigo Spirit at the National Convention Centre 11 January 2023
Getty Images

70
Quinn Rooney
The Victorious Australian Women's Cricket Team 2020
Getty Images

71
Hannah Peters
Australian Captain Meg Lanning Celebrates Winning the 2022 One-Day World Cup 2022
Getty Images

72
Dylan Burns
Lauren Pearce of the Demons and Caitlin Gould of the Crows Compete for the Ball during the 2022 AFLW Grand Final Match between the Adelaide Crows and the Melbourne Demons at Adelaide Oval 9 April 2022
Getty Images

73 See page 68

74
Bruce Howard (b.1936)
Sydney's Warwick Capper Taking a Spectacular Mark over Mick Martin of the Kangaroos in a Game at the MCG on Anzac Day 1991
Melbourne: Herald and Weekly Times, 1991
photograph, 40.5 x 29.4cm
Bruce Howard Collection of Photographs for *Herald and Weekly Times*, Melbourne, 1955–1995
nla.cat-vn3046135

75 See page 8

76
Photographer unknown
Portrait of Don Bradman c.1930s
photograph, 15.2 x 9.9cm
nla.cat-vn2998850

77
Steve Holland (b.1963)
Australian Cricketer Shane Warne at the End of the Fourth Test of the Ashes Series, Melbourne Cricket Ground 2006
digital photograph
nla.cat-vn4706559

78
Alex Davidson
Steve Smith Celebrates Double Century 2019
Getty Images

79
Michael Steele
Cadel Evans, Yellow Jersey Wearer of Team BMC Turns the Corner at L'Arc De Triomphe during the Twenty-First and Final Stage of Le Tour de France 2011
Getty Images

80
Rob Morrison
I Told You So
Strip Tees

81
Adam Petty
John Aloisi Kicks the Winning Penalty to Qualify Australia for the 2006 World Cup 2005
Getty Images

82–83
Tony Feder
Kerr's Trademark Backflip 2017
Getty Images

84 See page 74

85
Serena Ovens (b.1967)
Portrait of Louise Sauvage OAM, Atlanta 1996
gelatin silver photograph, 24.7 x 18.9cm
nla.cat-vn1430986

86
Christian Petersen
Lauren Jackson #15 of Australia Celebrates in the Second Half against Russia during the Women's Basketball Bronze Medal Game on Day 15 of the London 2012 Olympic Games 11 August 2012
Getty Images

87
Thomas Coex
Australia's Patty Mills Goes to the Basket in the Men's Bronze Medal Basketball Match between Slovenia and Australia during the Tokyo 2020 Olympic Games 7 August 2021
Getty Images

88
Clive Brunskill
Anna Meares of Australia Celebrates Winning the Gold Medal in the Women's Sprint Track Cycling Final on Day 11 of the London 2012 Olympic Games at the Velodrome, London 7 August 2012
Getty Images

89
Elsa Garrison
Dylan Alcott of Australia Celebrates with the Championship Trophy after Defeating Niels Vink of the Netherlands to Complete a 'Golden Slam' During Their Wheelchair Quad Singles Final Match on Day 14 of the 2021 US Open 12 September 2021
Getty Images

90
Jared C. Tilton
Minjee Lee of Australia Plays a Shot from the Bunker near the 14th Green during the Final Round of the 77th U.S. Women's Open 2022
Getty Images

91
Tim Clayton
Gold Medal Winner Emma McKeon of Australia after the Women's 50-metre Freestyle Final at the Tokyo Aquatic Centre during the Tokyo 2020 Olympic Games 1 August 2021
Getty Images

Published by National Library of Australia Publishing
Canberra ACT 2600

ISBN: 9781922507570

Contributing curators: Peter Appleton, Dr Grace Blakeley-Carroll, Dr Guy Hansen,
Shelly McGuire, Allister Mills, Dr Karen Schamberger
Publisher: Lauren Smith
Managing editor: Amelia Hartney
Editor: Dr Robert Nichols
Designer: Hugh Ford
Printed in Canberra, Australia, by CanPrint

The National Library of Australia thanks sports historian Bruce Coe for his contribution
to this book.

Find out more about NLA Publishing at nla.gov.au/national-library-publishing.

A catalogue record for this
book is available from the
National Library of Australia